a jarful of moonlight

nazanin mirsadeghi

Mirsadeghi, Nazanin
       a jarful of moonlight / Nazanin Mirsadeghi

Editor: Michael Loveday

ISBN-10: 1-939099-62-5
ISBN-13: 978-1-939099-62-4

a jarful of moonlight

one day
you will finally
meet yourself

and it will be love
at first sight

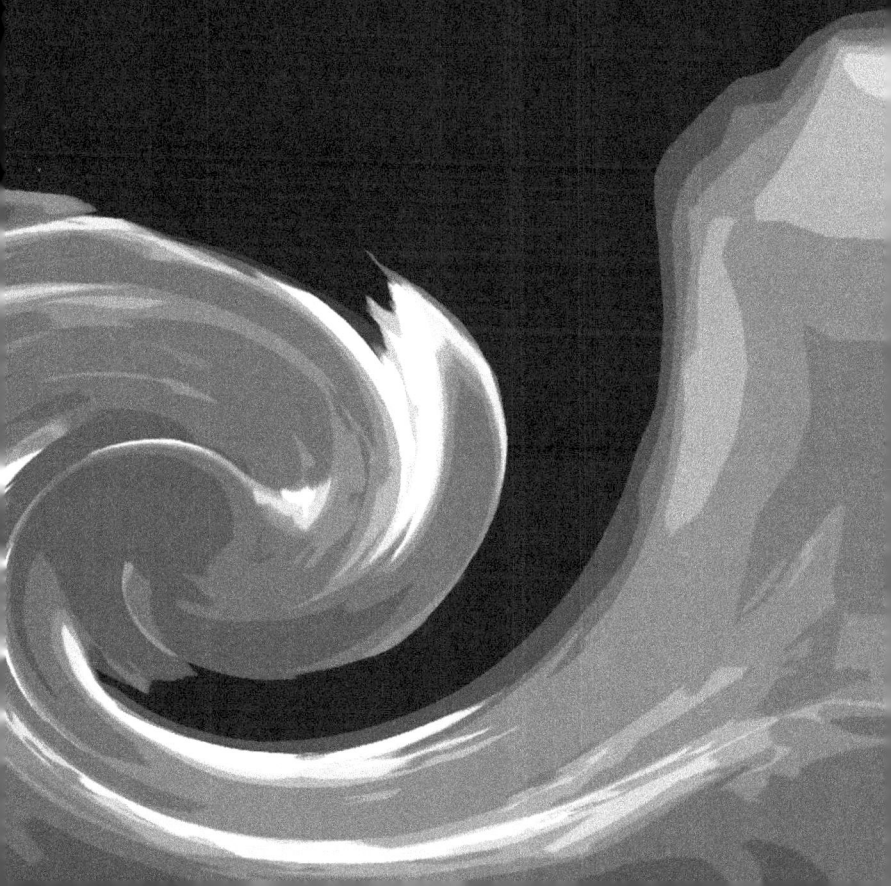

you grew on me
the way wild flowers grow on rock
turning all those rough edges
into something beautiful

your eyes
are the darkest ocean I know
each glance like a wave
pulls me into its undertow

and your smile
is the glimmer of a lighthouse
that every time
saves me from drowning

I come to you
with my open wounds
my broken dreams

you are my haven
a sacred place
to fall on my knees
and pray

in the darkness
sailing through
the waves of silky sheets,
my wrecked body drops anchor
next to yours
and my lips find sanctuary
in the warmth
of your gentle kisses

love is green
it knows how to grow
under a thick sheet of snow

dust of the earth
soil of the ground

here I am,

a piece of clay
in your creative hands

this poem that I heaved
from the bottom of my heart
I delicately recite
on the top of your lips
with a kiss

the heart of the lake
beats hard in his chest

he is in love with the moon!

can't you make a little bit
of room for me?

I just need a little space
for the seed of my love
to grow over time
in your heart

no name
no homeland
empty pockets
emptier hands

you are all I have

I weave a rope
made of soothing words
to pull the pain
out of your heart

hold on to me!

I will be
            your
                        driftwood!

I will
        carry you
                        to the
                                    shore!

I have grown
from this soil
I have opened my wings
in this sky
I have bloomed into spring
under this sun

and even though my roots
belong to another land

I am finding my voice
here, in this land
with you

I said nothing

I buried my face
in the palm of his hands
and wept

he is my homeland

he is the mist of morning breeze
in the street I used to walk

he is the taste of an orange pop
in my mouth
and its color on my lips
in a distant summer day

he is the navy blue shirt
I wore to school every day

he is all I packed in my suitcase
when I left
and the only piece of land
I hid in the palm of my hand
when I arrived

he is the language I speak
in my dreams

he is home

*can you hear
the sound of my shadow
cracking on the wall
when you pass me by?*

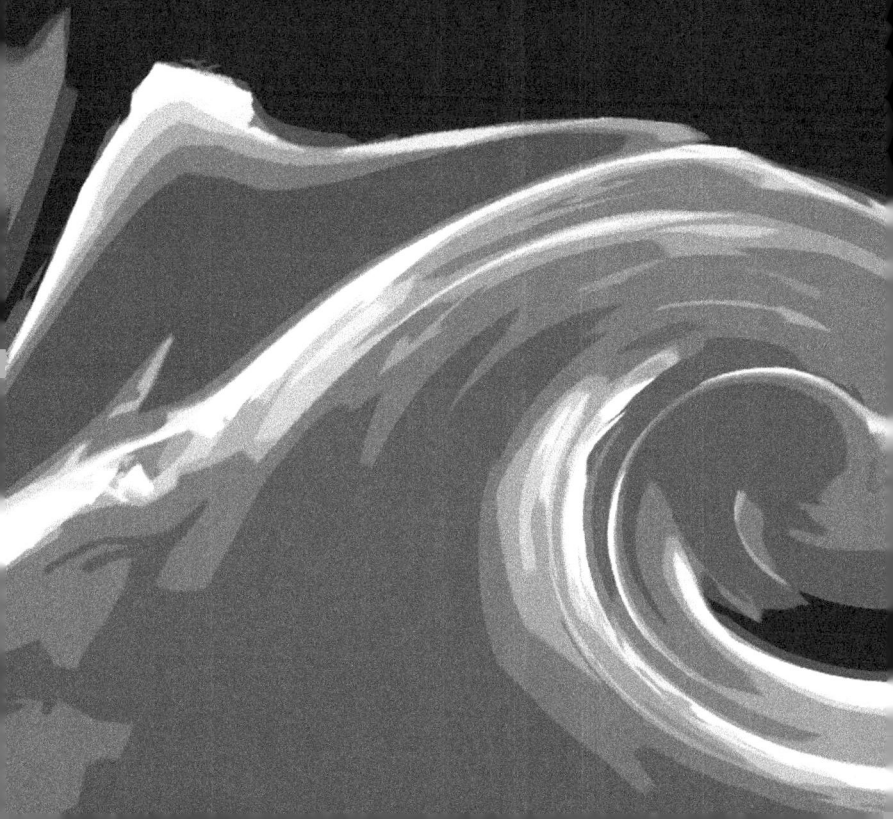

honed, razor-sharp
in the hands
of the merciless universe
that teaches you to cut
or be cut
you have become a blade

can you be water
with me, my love?
can you spare me
even for once?

the heart-shaped crystal
showcased behind the window
is flawlessly brilliant,
divinely elegant,
seductively out of reach,
and cold, cold, cold

open my chest!
a blood-red pomegranate
is beating inside!

I whisper your name
like a prayer
and breathe you in
like fresh air
I feel you run in my veins
and let you settle in my mind

I love you with all my being
but loving you
is not my being

I wish I could hold your heart
and shake it like a snow globe
so your feelings scatter around
like confetti

you have been standing still
for so long
that I can see nothing of you
behind
the tainted glass

you are my rock
you break me apart
you are my sun
you make me blind
you are my air
you leave me breathless

you are my world
my very, very, very
small world

tell me
this walk
on the edge of a cliff
waiting for rock
to crumble
under my feet
is not love

if love is 'falling'
I don't want to fall in love

I want to rise
I want to climb
I want to fly in love

he speaks love
in the bitter language
of lemon zest
and coffee beans

but he leaves
candy puffs
and cherry drops
under my pillow
as if they would turn
all my nightmares
into sweet dreams

I have washed
the hatred off the floor
I have wiped
the rage off the windows
I have cleaned
and swept
and dusted the animosity
from the house of my soul
all day long

so, take off the dirty shoes
of your cloudy mind
and tainted heart
before stepping
into my life tonight!

you take your heart
dark and black
no sugar,
no cream,
cold,
with plenty of ice

you take your heart
always to go

night
is burning up
its cracked lips
yearning for a drop of light

moon
fast asleep
deep
at the bottom of the well

do you remember
the *you* and *I*
in the faded picture
hanging on the wall?

we were free

we fell asleep
in the warm blanket
of each other's arms
and shared our meal
on the only plate we owned
life was simple
and we were rich

do you remember?

we used to break bread
with each other
now we break each other

I want to stretch my arms
and grow tall and green
covered with leaves
and sleeping buds
I want to bloom

you want me to stay
the way I am
a hopeless seed
under the soil
buried alive

I am
the dusty wind-up doll
on top of your music box

the dried pressed rose
between the pages of your almanac

the old bottle of wine
in the darkness of your cellar

but I wish, I wish, I wish
that I were just a dandelion
on the palms of your hands
waiting for a gentle wind
to carry me far
and set me free

she lives in a house
the house she always wanted

a big house where the wind
can embrace all four walls
and the trees
whisper in each other's ears

this was her dream
all she ever wished for

she lives in a house
a big house
and she sobs every night
on the shoulder of the trees
in the arms of the wind

cry out loud
let it out
before it grows
into a tangled knot
in your throat!

grief is a tightrope
stretched in time
from one horizon
to another

my heart is an acrobat
wavering in the air
stumbling in every step it takes
uncertain of finding peace
waiting at the end
with open arms

it knocked on the door
and I let it in

it sat on the sofa
drank my tea
sneaked into my bed
and held me so tight
that I couldn't breathe

it knocked on the door
and I let it in

pain is a sign

I'm still alive
if it hurts

my caring touch
and pouring love
will do nothing
to this bloomless tree

no matter how much I shine
no matter how long I rain
his wilted heart
won't turn green again

I stood at the doorstep
of our empty house
and watched you walk away

the maple trees
cried their most vibrant leaves
on your path,
and the fallen leaves
asked you to stay
though you crushed their hope
under your feet

I watched you walk away
without looking back
or thinking twice

you took the home
you took the green
with you
when you left

I was too much for you
too much sugar for your coffee
too much salt for your blood
too much heat for your heart

I was too much for you

you,
too little for me

the pain
you received as a gift
wrapped in a shiny paper
that said, *I love you!,*
you re-gifted to me
carefully wrapped in a shinier paper
that said, *I love you more!*

I am young
skin, soft
eyes, bright
bones, strong

I am old
soul, shattered
mind, twisted
spirit, cold

listen!
there is an ancient heart
inside my chest
that in every subtle beat
begs me to
stay alive
stay alive
stay alive

am I able
to stand any longer
with these cracks within my core
waiting for a gentle flick
to crumble me down
into a handful of
dust and sand?

holding my peace like a lantern
I tripped over a memory
and with the sound
of shattering glass
my world
plunged
into
darkness
again

come back to me
with the rain, the wind
or a dream
just come back

you are
a poet first

poems come
later

the pain
I carry
in my veins
will turn
into words
and the words
into poems

this is the way
healing
starts

remember,
only a never-typed
is free of typos

unearth the unwritten
poem
take your time

I soak my hands
in a mix of ink and honey
before I knead my words
to bake that fresh
loaf of poem

heat of a fire
glow of a flame
sizzling touch of an iron kiss

my heart
is branded by a poem

I have a word to sow
I water it
with moonlight

then
I sit and watch it grow
into a poem

last night
I went for a walk
and I came back with
a jarful of moonlight

I was running out of honey!

standing tall

her feet
rooted in the core of the soil
and her hands
buried in the lightness of the clouds

her body becomes
                    a bridge
                         between
                              heaven
                                   and
                                      earth!

trying to stay alive
gasping for air
I put up a fight
before I drown

then, I realize
to my surprise
that I am
a fish!

a room
lit up by the rays
of the moon

a figure
blended in the shadows
on the wall

a woman
a crib
and a sleeping child

for Neema

when he lost his first tooth
he asked the Tooth Fairy
for a fishing rod

we never went out fishing

he sailed his imaginary boat
all day long
catching make-believe words
from the sea below his bed
to write a story about a boy
who loved to fish
all day long

she loves to make a big crown
out of bubbles
loaded with precious gems that shine
under the fluorescent light

she is the queen of bathtub land!

but tonight,
she leaned her little body back
– her skinny arms holding her weight –
held her long curly hair
under the running water
and stayed still

what are you doing?
                       I asked
I am a flower,
             she smiled
I am watering myself to grow fast

you were that little girl
whose fingertips
were always covered in ink
and the number of the books she read
was greater than the words she said

you were that little girl
whose favorite color
was not pink, or purple
or even blue
it was yellow, and it was brown
because she was madly in love
with the autumn leaves

you were that little girl
who was neither a princess
nor a tomboy
who never learned to dance
or kick a ball

the little girl
who was alone but not lonely
and always carried sweet words
in the pocket of her skirt
to share with those
who had a bitter day

you are that little girl
that after all these years
every one still remembers
when all the pinks and purples
and even blues
are long forgotten